The Wedding Guide
"Simple and Straight to the Point"

Rose White Brown

DEDICATION

To all Ministers in Training, Pastors , Leaders, Notaries and all those responsible for make the lives of couples preparing for marriage a memorable moment.

CONTENTS

Preface

This manual is meant to be used as a companion to the Bible. It alone may be adequate for use in certain services, such as in some weddings and funerals, but is not meant to be a substitute for the Bible. Additional passages are usually suggested which may be read from the Bible itself. Several versions of the Bible are used and are designated.

The book is outlined by sections so that the materials desired may be easily located. At the beginning of each chapter certain guiding principles are set forth as practical aids in approaching a particular area of ministry. In many churches it is understood that ministers are not bound to any particular ritual. It is suggested that the individual minister study these principles and orders of service, together with other resource materials, and then plan his own order of service. By following this procedure, the minister has the treasures of Christian history as resources, and at the same time he may use his own creative imagination in making his ministry contemporary and relevant.

No particular originality is claimed for this manual. Many resources have been drawn upon in this production. The aim has been to make it as contemporary in language and spirit as possible.

This manual for conducting wedding ceremonies has grown out of a background of over thirty-five years of ministry in local churches and eleven years of teaching young ministers both as a ministry coach as well as in schools of ministry. I have attempted to produce the kind of practical manual that was desired for my own ministry through the years. Actually, it has been approximately twenty years in the making. I am indebted to many pastors as well as colleagues in the teaching ministry for many of these materials. With this brief introduction and explanation, the manual is offered with a prayer that fellow ministers in the Lord may find helpful and that God may see fit to place His blessings upon its ministry.

1 WEDDINGS

"Let marriage be held in honor among all."

(Hebrews 13:4)

One of the preacher's chief joys is to help a fine Christian couple arrange their wedding and establish their home. Our Lord performed His first miracle at the marriage in Cana of Galilee. Let us, as His servants, bring Christ's living presence into each wedding we conduct. Several forms are included in this manual. Confer with the prospective bride and groom and guide them in selecting that which will best express their pledges of love and commitment.

A couple may delete parts of a ceremony, or they may choose to combine selections from several. In every case, their ceremony should reflect the sacred covenant represented as well as satisfy the civil requirements.

One of the preacher's first duties in a new location is to contact the local authorities, usually in the Court House, and register with them so that he may properly perform marriages. In arranging the wedding, respect the bride's wishes as far as possible. Much contemporary music is as beautiful and appropriate as the traditional. Selected poetry or quotations may be included with good effect. Encourage the couple to keep their wedding simple.

Money that might be better used for setting up housekeeping can easily be spent on an extravagant ceremony and reception. A wedding need not be lavish to be memorable. When the bride wishes to have a visiting preacher perform her wedding, courtesy will be shown if she first discusses this with the local preacher and includes him. The two preachers can meet and make arrangements according to her wishes, each of them taking part in the ceremony. If a priest is to be asked, this invitation, too, is extended by the local preacher, and the priest will participate in the wedding under his direction.

Acquaint the bride with what is available from the church for her use: candelabras? An aisle cloth? Flower stands?

Who will play the organ or piano? Will there be a soloist? If the reception is to be held in the church, what is available? Does the church have tea service? A punch bowl? Wedding decorations? Who will serve? Is there a charge for using the building? Will this include the reception? Organist? Custodian? The preacher may wish to meet with the couple for more than one session, not only to discuss the wedding, but to go into other matters as well. In the rare situation where the preacher cannot in good conscience perform a wedding, they should tell the couple so, and tell them why. The final decision as to whether they should perform the wedding or not must always rest with the preacher, and in such cases they must be true to their conscience before God; suggestions for pre-marital counseling are given later on in this manual.

A wedding with processional, music, and several attendants requires a complete rehearsal in order that, on the day of the ceremony, participants can concentrate upon the sacred union taking place rather than wondering where to stand or what to do.

Ask the bride and groom to notify all members of the wedding party concerning the time of the rehearsal, which will require one hour at the church. If there is to be a rehearsal dinner, the dinner should be scheduled afterward. The rehearsal should provide a complete acting out of the wedding ceremony, though singing may be omitted, with all matters clearly understood by the entire company, the organist, the ushers, and the parents. A second *"walk-through"* to the music, and going through the movements but not the vows, will further enable the wedding party to carry out their responsibilities properly. It will also be helpful if the ushers *"walk-through"* all of their responsibilities. These include lighting the candles, seating the groom's parents and bride's mother, unrolling the aisle cloth, and then taking their places with the wedding party to begin the procession.

Marriage is one of life's primary experiences. The Christian wedding is a historic ceremony of dedication administered by the church and a ritual of commitment for those entering into marriage. In it God's blessings are invoked by the minister and the congregation.

It is a celebration of God's establishment of the home as the primary social institution. The planning and performance of the wedding ceremony should therefore be carried out with seriousness, dignity, and joy.

2 GUIDIING PRINCIPLES

1. Since a wedding involves many persons, the church should provide a wholesome atmosphere and a complete program of education in which youth may rightly mature in the matters of dating, becoming engaged, and planning for establishing Christian homes.

2. Prior to the wedding the minister should counsel the couple concerning such matters as the basic responsibility of commitment in a maturing relationship, vocation and home finances, mutual fulfilment in sexual relationships, planning for children, and the relation of the home to the church. The planning of the wedding as to the kind (formal or informal) and time and place (church or home), and procedures for the rehearsal and the wedding ceremony should be agreed upon. The minister should make certain the couple understands the requirements of the law regarding marriage.

The pastor may wish to give them a copy of a good book on marriage, such as Woods's Harmony in Marriage or David Mace's Success in Marriage.

3. Laws governing marriage and divorce are under the authority of the state and vary from state to state. The

minister should familiarize himself with the laws of his state. A proper marriage license is uniformly required. Some states require a waiting period after the license is acquired. Blood tests (Wassermann or its equivalent) are required in most states. Some states require a minister to be ordained and to register with the court clerk. Immediately following the wedding the minister should fill in the marriage license, sign it, and promptly mail it personally to the office which issued it. He may provide the couple with a certificate of marriage.

4. Appropriate music should be chosen. Ordinary popular music should be avoided. Good hymns are often used today and may be sung by the congregation.

Processionals (hymns may be sung by congregation)

"For the Beauty of the Earth"

"God of Our Fathers, Whose Almighty Hand"

"Praise, My Soul, the King of Heaven"

"Praise the Lord! Ye Heavens, Adore Him"

"Praise to God, Immortal Praise"

"Praise to the Lord, the Almighty"

"We, Thy People, Praise Thee"

"Bride's Chorus" from Lohengrin by Wagner

Recessionals (hymns may be sung by congregation)

"Joyful, Joyful, We Adore Thee"

"Love Divine, All Loves Excelling"

"Now Thank We All Our God"

"O Master, Let Me Walk with Thee"

"Wedding March" by Mendelssohn

Wedding Hymns (may be used as an organ or vocal selection)

"Lord, Who at Cana's Wedding Feast"

"May the Grace of Christ Our Saviour"

"O Father, All Creating"

"O Love Divine and Golden"

"O Perfect Love"

"The King of Love My Shepherd Is"

Organ Music

"Arioso in A Major"; "Jesu, Joy of Man's Desiring";

"Sheep May Safely Graze"; "Sinfonia" from Wedding Cantata (Bach)

"Cantabile" (Franck)

Slow Movements from Violin Concertos (Handel; Arr., Klein)

"Love Dream" (Liszt)

"Aria" (Peters)

"Serenade" (Schubert)

"Carillon" (Sowerby)

"Prelude on 'Rhosymedre' " (Vaughan Williams)

"Marriage at Cana in Galilee" (Weinberger)

Vocal Music

"Be Thou But Near"; "Jesus Shepherd, Be Near Me";

"My Heart Ever Faithful"; "O Love That Casts Out Fear" (Bach)

"I Love You Truly" (Bond)

"Though I Speak with Tongues" (Brahms)

"O Perfect Love" (Burleigh)

"True Love Is God's Gift" (Chambers)

"Because" (d'Hardelot)

"A Wedding Prayer" (Dunlap)

"The Twenty-third Psalm"; "I Will Sing New Songs of Gladness" (Dvorak)

"O Lord Most Holy" (Franck)

"The Song of Ruth" (Gounod)

"Wedding Hymn" (Handel)

"A Wedding Benediction"; "We Lift Our Hearts to Thee" (Lovelace)

"Eternal Love" (Willan)

5. Etiquette is important in weddings. For example, the minister should dress in keeping with that of the wedding party. For the informal wedding an ordinary street suit of dark blue, dark gray, or black, with black shoes, white shirt, and dark accessories is appropriate. For the formal wedding, if the party wears tuxedos, the minister may wear a tuxedo or a cut-away dark gray morning coat and vest, with gray and black striped trousers, white shirt with turned-down collar and black or black and gray ascot tie. If the wedding party wears full-dress (tails,

standing or wing collar, white shirt with studs, white bow tie and white gloves), the minister may wear the same, or he may wear a robe.

6. Printed instructions, adopted by the church, concerning the use of church facilities may be given to those planning for weddings.

7. There should be no taking of flash pictures during the processional, the ceremony, or the recessional. They may be taken afterwards, before or during the reception.

3 THE REHEARSAL

Begin the rehearsal by asking the bride and groom to come forward and take their places in front of the preacher. The bride is to the preacher's right as they face the audience; the groom to his left. Ask the bride to place her attendants as follows: *maid of honor, matron of honor* (in that order if there are both), *then the bridesmaids. Ask the groom to station his best man next to him and then the groomsmen.*

Some brides like to arrange the couples according to height. Having the bride and groom name the order of their attendants is better than leaving this responsibility to the preacher. Position the flower girl near the maid of honor, who can direct the little girl if need be. Likewise, position the ring bearer near the best man. Consideration should be given to the most advantageous placement of the wedding party within the space and design of the sanctuary.

If there are steps to a raised platform, usually the early part of the ceremony takes place on the floor level, the, at the point where the vows are to be exchanged, the participants move to the platform. Where steps are off to one side this may not be practical. Some brides prefer to have only the wedding couple, the maid of honor and best man, and the ring bearer and flower girl accompany the preacher to the platform. Other brides choose to have the entire wedding party move forward into a tiered arrangement with the outermost attendants on the first step, and the succeeding attendants each on the next higher step until the pyramid comes together on the platform with the wedding couple, best man and maid of honor, ring bearer and flower girl, and the preacher. Both arrangements may be rehearsed and the bride may choose which she prefers. These diagrams are intended as guides to deciding upon the best placement of the wedding party:

4 ARRANGEMENTS

ARRANGEMENT #1

BF

U...U...U...BM...G...B...MH...Bm...Bm...Bm

RB......P...... FG

ARRANGEMENT #1

U...U...U...U   BF...Bm...Bm...Bm...Bm

BM...G....B

MH

RB…..………P……..FG

CODE

U-Usher   G-Groom   BF-Bride's Father

MH-Maid *(Matron)* of Honor

B-Bride   P-Preacher   Bm-Bridesmaid

BM-Best Man   RB-Ring Bearer   FG-Flower Girl

During the rehearsal, assure the bride and groom that, during the ceremony, the preacher will prompt their responses, instructing them what to say and what movements to make, *such as during the ring ceremony, lighting the unity candle, and so forth.* All vows should be rehearsed, though the responses need not be made. Likewise, all movements: *such as coming to the platform, the ring exchange, lighting the unity candle, and kneeling if the couple chooses to kneel.*

5 PLANNING THE WEDDING

Most couples who come to a preacher to plan their weddings want a formal wedding, but there are many forms that weddings can take. Help the couple choose from the following elements those that they want to be included in their ceremony, and how each will be done. Whether the wedding party is to dress at home or at the church building, all participants should be ready at the church one hour before the ceremony begins.

The auditorium should be prepared before the rehearsal. If the reception is to be in the church fellowship hall that room should also be prepared the day before, if possible, or at least before any of the guests arrive.

The music usually begins thirty minutes before the ceremony itself begins. Instrumental or a mixture of instrumental and vocal music can be used.

Two ushers light the candles as soon as the music begins. If the ceremony will include lighting a unity candle, the ushers will light the two outer candles required at the same time they light the candles in the candelabras, or the mothers will light them at the time they are seated. The center candle is left unlit until the bride and groom light it in the unity ceremony. The guest book is placed near the entrance door and guests may sign before coming into the sanctuary. Ushers will greet the guests at the door of the sanctuary after they have signed the guest book, and will take them to their seats.

The bride's guests are seated in the left half of the auditorium, and the groom's on the right.

However, when the wedding is held at a distance from the groom's home and he can expect fewer guests, ushers should distribute the guests evenly rather than have most seated in the bride's section.

The usher offer their right arm to the lady when she is accompanied by her escort; to the older of two women who have come together. If a man comes alone, an usher takes him to his seat, walking beside him on the left. The front pews are reserved for family members of the wedding couple. Grandparents and other close family members will be seated in the second and third pews *(more if necessary)* on either side according to their relationship to the bride and groom. Brothers and sisters of the wedding couple who are not participating in the ceremony may sit in the first pew with the parents.

If there is no railing enclosing the front pews, the parents actually sit in the second pew, grandparents in the third, and so forth. Minutes before the ceremony begins, the groom's parents will be seated, an usher giving their right arm to the mother and leading her, with the father two steps behind, to the center aisle in the first pew on the right side.

The bride's mother will be seated last, ushered to the center aisle seat in the first pew on the bride's side *(the left, facing the altar)*.

Some brides prefer to have the candles lighted just before the bride's mother is seated, in which case the groom's mother must be seated early enough that lighting the candles and unrolling the aisle cloth not delay the ceremony. When there is no center aisle, the right aisle may be treated as if it were a center aisle, with the wedding taking place at the head of this aisle. Parents and guests are seated on either side of this aisle, and the remaining sections of the auditorium are ignored.

If the bride expects the building to be filled, she may prefer to divide the front pews with a decorative ribbon and have the parents sit on either side of this front pew, grandparents in the second pew, and so forth. The left side of the building becomes the bride's side, the right the groom's. Divorced parents do not occupy the same pew. The groom's mother will be seated in the first pew with the groom's stepfather, and the groom's father will take his seat earlier in the third row with his wife, behind the groom's grandparents.

Likewise, the bride's mother takes the aisle seat in the first row, with her husband if she is married.

The bride's father, not the stepfather, brings his daughter

down the aisle, and after giving her away, he takes his seat in the third row on the bride's side.

Following the seating of the bride's mother, two ushers unroll the aisle cloth, and then retire to join the wedding party, and the ceremony is ready to begin. Any guests who arrive after that should be seated from side aisles. When the organist begins the processional, the preacher, groom, best man, and groomsmen enter in that order, either from behind the altar of coming down a side aisle. The preacher stands at the head of the center aisle, facing the audience; the groom stands just to his left and nearer the first pew, with the best man and groomsmen aligned behind him parallel to the front pew. The bridesmaids proceed slowly down the center aisle, one at a time. The farthest bridesmaid enters first, then nearer bridesmaids, with the maid of honor last.

The ring bearer followers; then the flower girl. As the organist strikes the wedding march, the bride enters, upon the right arm of her father.

Her mother stands as a signal to the congregation that they also stand and remain standing as the bride comes down the aisle. The bride may prefer to have the groomsmen and bridesmaids enter in pairs, separating as they approach the altar to take their places. In this case, the preacher, groom, and best man enter first. The attendants then enter in pairs; then the maid of honor, ring bearer, flower girl, and the bride with her father. The bride remains with her father until the preacher asks, *"Who is giving this woman to be married to this man?"* After his reply, the bride's father retires to his seat next to the bride's mother. If there is no center aisle, the procession may go up the left aisle and the wedding party exit down the right aisle after the ceremony.

6 THE CEREMONY

The ceremony itself may involve a variety of elements. Several of these are listed below in the order they usually occur. You or the couple may think of others, also. Notice how each of the following elements is used in the model ceremonies on pages 94 – 106. Then build the ceremony that best suits the wishes of the bride and groom:

1. Statement of Purpose
2. Declaration of Consent/Intent
3. The Giving of the Bride
4. Exhortation to the Bride and Groom
5. The Marriage Vows
6. Reading of Scripture
7. The Exchange of Rings
8. Lighting the Unity Candle
9. Prayer for the Bride and Groom
10. The Pronouncement of Marriage
11. The Nuptial Kiss
12. Recognition of Parents
13. Benediction

14. Presentation of the Newlyweds

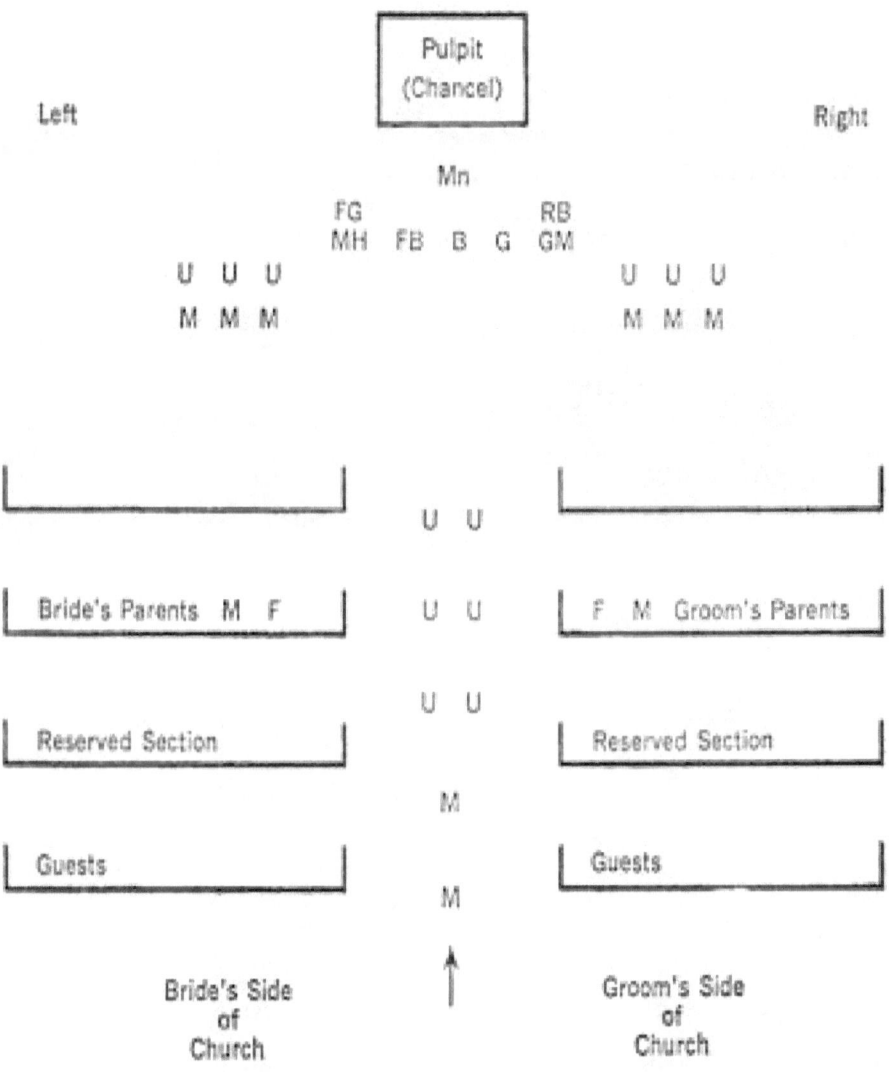

Key to Diagram

B—Bride

MH—Maid of Honor

M—Maid

FG—Flower Girl

MB—Mother of Bride

FB—Father of Bride

Mn—Minister

G—Groom

GM—Groomsman

U—Usher

RB—Ring Bearer

MG—Mother of Groom

FG—Father of Groom

Certain general elements should be included, such as (1) the purpose of the gathering, (2) the meaning of marriage, (3) the charge to the couple, (4) questions to the bride and groom, (5) the affirming of commitments, (6) the pronouncement of the marriage, and (7) a prayer of petition and dedication asking God's blessings upon the newly established home.

The following ceremony for a formal wedding may serve as a guide for the minister who constructs his own ceremony, or it may be used as it is if he desires.

Certain parts of the ceremony, such as repeating the phrase "With this ring I pledge" and so forth, may be omitted. Some couples prefer a briefer ceremony.

The minister will use his own discretion as to the length, as long as it is reasonably brief and the essential elements are included. The ceremony may be read or it may be repeated from memory. The entire ceremony, including the processional and the recessional, usually takes ten to twenty minutes.

MINISTER: Dear friends [or dearly beloved, or beloved friends], we are here assembled in the presence of God to unite A___[groom's name] and B___[bride's name] in marriage.

The Bible teaches that marriage is to be a permanent relationship of one man and one woman freely and totally committed to each other as companions for life. Our Lord declared that man shall leave his father and mother and unite with his wife in the building of a home, and the two shall become one flesh.

Who gives the bride to be married?

BRIDE'S FATHER: I do [or he may say, "Her mother

and I"].

MINISTER: The home is built upon love, which virtue is best portrayed in the thirteenth chapter of Paul's first letter to the Corinthians. "Love is patient and kind; love is not jealous or boastful; it is not arrogant or rude. Love does not insist on its own way; it is not irritable or resentful; it does not rejoice at wrong, but rejoices in the right. Love bears all things, believes all things, hopes all things, endures all things. Love never ends; … So faith, hope, love abide, these three; but the greatest of these is love" [*1 Cor. 13:4–13, RSV*].

Marriage is a companionship which involves mutual commitment and responsibility. You will share alike in the responsibilities and the joys of life. When companions share a sorrow the sorrow is halved, and when they share a joy the joy is doubled.

You are exhorted to dedicate your home to your Creator. Take his Word, the Bible, for your guide. Give loyal devotion to his church, thus uniting the mutual strength of these two most important institutions, living your lives as his willing servants, and true happiness will be your temporal and eternal reward.

Let us pray. O Lord of life and love, bestow thy grace upon this marriage, and seal this commitment of thy children with thy love.

As thou hast brought them together by thy divine

providence, sanctify them by thy Spirit, that they may give themselves fully one to the other and to thee. Give them strength and patience to live their lives in a manner that will mutually bless themselves and honor thy holy name, through Jesus Christ our Lord. Amen.

(The minister will ask them to join their right hands and take the following vows):

MINISTER TO GROOM: A____, will you take B_____ to be your wife; will you commit yourself to her happiness and her self-fulfilment as a person, and to her usefulness in God's kingdom; and will you promise to love, honor, trust, and serve her in sickness and in health, in adversity and prosperity, and to be true and loyal to her, so long as you both shall live?

GROOM: I will.

MINISTER TO BRIDE: B___, will you take A____ to be your husband; will you commit yourself to his happiness and his self-fulfillment as a person, and to his usefulness in God's kingdom; and do you promise to love, honor, trust, and serve him in sickness and in health, in adversity and prosperity, and to be true and loyal to him, so long as you both shall live?

BRIDE: I will.

(If the wedding ring is to be used, the bride will hand her bouquet to the maid of honor when the ceremony

starts. The engagement ring will be left at home or transferred to the right hand prior to the processional. The minister will receive the ring from the groomsman and proceed.)

MINISTER: The wedding ring is a symbol of marriage in at least two ways: the purity of gold symbolizes the purity of your love for each other, and the unending circle symbolizes the unending vows which you are taking, which may be broken honorably in the sight of God only by death. As a token of your vows, you will give and receive the ring [*or rings*].

MINISTER TO GROOM: A___, you will give the ring and repeat after me: B___, with this ring I pledge my life and love to you, in the name of the Father, and of the Son, and of the Holy Spirit." [*The Groom repeats this.*]

MINISTER TO BRIDE: B___, you will give the ring and repeat after me: "A___, with this ring I pledge my love and life to you, in the name of the Father, and of the Son, and of the Holy Spirit." [*The Bride repeats this.*]

(In the case of a single ring ceremony, the bride will say, "A___, I accept this ring and pledge to you my love and life, in the name of the Father, and of the Son, and of the Holy Spirit.")

MINISTER: Will both of you please repeat after me:

Entreat me not to leave you

or to return from following you;

for where you go I will go,

and where you lodge I will lodge;

your people shall be my people,

and your God my God [*Ruth 1:16, RSV*].

[*The Couple repeats this.*]

MINISTER TO CONGREGATION: Since they have made these commitments before God and this assembly [*or, these witnesses*], by the authority of God and the laws of this state, I declare that A___and B___are husband and wife.

MINISTER TO COUPLE: A___and B___, you are no longer two independent persons but one. "What therefore God has joined together, let no man separate" [*Matt. 19:6, NASB*].

(The bride and groom may now kneel, and the minister may express a free prayer. Or the Model Prayer (Matt. 6:9–14, KJV) may be repeated by the minister and the bride and groom, or by the entire congregation.)

Our Father which art in heaven, Hallowed be thy name.

Thy kingdom come. Thy will be done in earth, as it is

in heaven.

Give us this day our daily bread.

And forgive us our debts, as we forgive our debtors.

And lead us not into temptation, but deliver us from evil:

For thine is the kingdom, and the power, and the glory, forever. Amen.

(The minister may then add the benediction; it may either be one of his own composition or a passage of Scripture, such as one of those given below.)

The Lord bless you and keep you:

The Lord make his face to shine upon you, and be gracious to you:

The Lord lift up his countenance upon you, and give you peace [*Num. 6:24–26, RSV*].

The grace of the Lord Jesus Christ and the love of God and the fellowship of the Holy Spirit be with you all [*2 Cor. 13:14, RSV*]. Amen.

7 The Informal Wedding

The bride and her family may prefer an informal wedding in their home, in the home of the minister, in the church chapel, or in the minister's study. The couple may wish to be accompanied by their parents only or by a few friends. The informal wedding ceremony is usually somewhat briefer than the formal ceremony. It includes all of the essentials of a ceremony, particularly the taking of vows and the pronouncement of the marriage. Certain lines ordinarily repeated after the minister may be omitted.

In any case, the ceremony should be conducted reverently and with dignity.

Suggested Informal Ceremony

The following brief ceremony may be used in the informal wedding. The wedding party will assemble informally. The minister will take his stand and indicate where the bride and groom will stand, and their attendants also, if there are any. The ceremony will then proceed.

MINISTER: Friends, we are assembled here to unite

A_____ and B_____ in marriage. The Bible teaches that marriage is of divine origin. The home is God's gift to man.

Marriage is a commitment which one man and one woman make to each other and to God. The vows you are about to make should be kept seriously as long as you both live.

MINISTER TO COUPLE: A_____ and B_____, you will now join your right hands together and make the following vows.

MINISTER TO GROOM: A_____, will you take B_____ to be your lawful wife, and will you promise to love, honor, and support her, keeping only to her, as long as you both live?

GROOM: I will.

MINISTER TO BRIDE: B_____, will you take A_____to be your lawful husband, and will you promise to love, honor, and cooperate with him, keeping only to him, as long as you both live?

BRIDE: I will.

MINISTER: Since you have made these vows, by the authority of the state and as a minister of the gospel of Jesus Christ, I now pronounce that you are husband and wife. Whom God has joined together, let not man separate.

(Prayer for God's blessings upon the marriage.)

The minister will congratulate the couple. If there is to be no reception, the family and friends will also offer their congratulations at this time.

Note: For further instructions sec Amy Vanderbilt, *Etiquette*; Emily Post, *Etiquette*; Mrs. Burton Kingsland, *The Book of Weddings*; May Detherage, *Planning Your Wedding*; Elizabeth Swadley, *Your Christian Wedding*.

8 The Home Wedding

When the wedding is held in the home of the bride, the plan suggested for the formal wedding at the church may be used, with certain necessary adjustments. The bride's mother will stand at the door and greet the guests, and the groom's parents will be seated with other friends.

An improvised altar may be constructed inside the home or on the lawn. The minister, groom, and the best man enter through one door and the bridal party through another. If there is a stairway the bridal party usually enters from there. A processional may be played. There is no recessional. Following the benediction, the minister should extend his best wishes for their happiness and congratulate the groom. Friends may then gather about them to offer their congratulations.

9 The Renewal of Vows

A service for renewal of vows may be requested by married couples at wedding anniversaries or upon other significant occasions. This is particularly fitting for the golden wedding anniversary conducted in the home.

A renewal service may also be conducted at a regular worship service when all married couples will renew their vows as an emphasis upon the Christian home.

The minister may read an appropriate passage of Scripture, emphasizing the importance of the home. He then may use the following ceremony.

MINISTER: Friends, we are here assembled in the presence of God to witness the renewal of the marriage vows taken by this couple, A_____ and B_____ [*or, these couples*], when they were united in holy marriage. God is always pleased when we rededicate our lives and our homes by an act of worship.

(The minister may add any other thoughts appropriate to the particular situation.)

MINISTER: You will now please unite your right hands.

Do you now promise to renew the vows which you made when you were first united in marriage?

COUPLE [*or couples*]: We do.

MINISTER: Do you promise to continue to keep the vows and the covenant which you made at your wedding?

COUPLE: We do.

MINISTER: Do you promise to continue to cultivate your love for each other by discipline, understanding, trustfulness, compassion, thoughtfulness, patience, and mutual consideration?

COUPLE: We do.

MINISTER: Do you promise to endeavor to create a Christian environment in your home and to help each other to live godly lives in Christian service?

COUPLE: We do.

MINISTER: Because of the vows which you have renewed with each other and with God in the presence of these witnesses, let us now join in a prayer of dedication.

(The minister will now pray for the couple or couples, for the home, for the church, and for the kingdom of God.)

Following the prayer, a hymn of thanksgiving and

praise to God may be sung by the company present. The entire order of service may be planned with creative imagination for the good of all concerned.

10 THE RECESSIONAL & DISMISSAL OF GUESTS

When the ceremony is over, the bride and groom will leave first, to be followed by the best man and maid of honor, the groomsmen and bridesmaids, and the ring bearer and flower girl, all in pairs. An usher returns immediately for the bride's mother and father. A second usher comes for the groom's parents. Then two ushers come together and, beginning at the front pew, dismiss the guests one row at a time.

11 THE RECEIVING LINE

The order for a formal receiving line is as follows: *bride's mother, father of the groom, mother of the groom, father of the bride, bride, groom, matron of honor, maid of honor, and bridesmaids according to age.*

 If guests are to be received informally after the ceremony, this arrangement may be preferred: *the bride and groom stand together in the center of the receiving line, with the bride's parents next to her, the groom's parents next to him. Bridesmaids take their places to the bride's left at the beginning of the receiving line, the groomsmen to the groom's right at the end, except for the two ushers who will be dismissing the guests.*

The maid of honor will precede the bride's parents, the best man will stand following the groom's parents. In the case of divorced parents, the bride may prefer to have only her mother stand with her in the receiving line.

12 PICTURES

Pictures may be taken and the wedding recorded without distracting from the ceremony. The photographer should keep himself as inconspicuous as possible. Ordinarily, no flashes are permitted during prayer; but some pastors refuse to permit photographs during any of the ceremony. Wedding pictures may be posed following the ceremony and greeting of the guests. When the reception immediately follows, the couple should cut the cake first in order that their guests may be served while these pictures are being staged.

13 A BRIEF CEREMONY

- <u>STATEMENT OF PURPOSE</u> – Marriage is as old as the family of man. It was given by our Creator in the Garden of Eden in the state of innocence. Moses, the great lawgiver of Israel, first gave legal sanction, and our Lord Jesus Christ, when He was upon the earth, gave it spiritual sanction. Rightly regarded, marriage is the highest and happiest of human relationships, the preserver of true love, the foundation of the home, and the strength of society. The Scriptures teach us that marriage should *"be held in honor among all."* If you have both duly considered this relationship upon which you are about to enter, please indicate by joining your right hands.

THE MARRIAGE VOWS

TO GROOM: *G_____ _____, * do you take this woman, whose right hand you now hold, to be your wedded wife, and do you promise before God and these witnesses that you will be to her a true and devoted husband; true to her in sickness and in health, in joy and sorrow, in prosperity and I adversity; and that forsaking all others you will keep yourself to her, and to her only, until God shall separate you by death? If so, answer "I*

DO."

TO BRIDE: *B*_____ _____, * *do you take this man, whose right hand you now hold, to be your wedded husband, and do you promise before God and these witnesses that you will be to him a true and devoted wife; true to him in sickness and in health, in joy and in sorrow, in prosperity and in adversity;*

and that forsaking all others you will keep yourself to him, and to him only, until God shall separate you by death? If so, answer "I DO."

*G_____ _____ shall indicate the groom's full name; G_____ shall indicate just his first name. B_____ _____ shall indicate the bride's full name; B_____, her first name.

THE EXCHANGE OF RINGS

If a ring (or rings) will be used, the pastor shall say:

May this golden circle, the emblem of an untarnished eternity, be the sign and seal of a pure and imperishable faith you have now pledged to each other. *The pastor will give the ring to the groom, who will then place it upon the third finger of the bride's left hand. The pastor shall then continue:*

THE PRONOUNCEMENT OF MARRIAGE

Therefore, by virtue of the authority vested in me as a minister of the Gospel of Jesus Christ, and in accordance with the laws of God and the sovereign State of_____, I now pronounce you husband and wife-one in name, one in aim, and one, we trust, in a happy destiny. *"What God has put together, let no man pull asunder."*

PRAYER FOR THE BRIDE & GROOM

"Our Father, we thank You for the joy of living, and especially for the joys of love and marriage. You have loved us, and You have made us so that we can love and be loved in return. Thank You that we need not walk the road alone, but that You provide someone to share our dreams and comfort us in our sorrows. Father bless these Your children today as they begin their lives together as husband and wife. Preserve and protect this love they have expressed. May the know happiness and fulfillment; may the experience contentment and peace. As they come to know each other better, may they also learn to know You, so that their home becomes a beacon to others of that life and joy which are eternal. In Jesus' name we pray; Amen!

14 THE TRADITIONAL MARRIAGE SERVICE

- <u>STATEMENT OF PURPOSE</u> – *"Dearly beloved: We have come together in the presence of God to witness the joining together of this man and this woman in holy matrimony. The sacred relationship of marriage was established by God in creation, and our Lord Jesus Christ adorned marriage by His presence and first miracle at the wedding in Cana of Galilee. The Apostle Paul chose marriage to symbolize the union between Christ and His church, and Holy Scripture commends marriage to be honored among all people. The union of husband and wife in heart, body, and mind is intended by God for their mutual joy; for the help and comfort given to one another in prosperity and adversity; and, when it is God's will, for the procreation of children and their nurture in the knowledge and love of the Lord. Therefore, marriage is not to be entered into unadvisedly or lightly, but soberly, deliberately, and in reverent fear before God. In this holy union, G_____ and B_____ now come to be joined.*

DECLARATION OF CONSENT

TO GROOM: *G_____ _____, will you have this woman to be your wife; to live together in the holy covenant of marriage? Will you love her, comfort her, honor and keep her, in sickness and in health, and, forsaking all others, be faithful to her so long as you both shall live? If so, answer, "I WILL."*

TO BRIDE: *B_____ _____, will you have this man to be your husband; to live together in the holy covenant of marriage? Will you love him, comfort him, honor and keep him, in sickness and in health, and forsaking all others, be faithful to him so long as you both shall live? If so, answer, "I WILL."*

TO CONGREGATION: *Will all of you witnessing these promises do all in your power to uphold these two persons in their marriage? If so, please answer, "We will."*

THE GIVING OF THE BRIDE

TO THE BRIDE'S FATHER: *Who is giving this woman to be married to this man? The bride's father answers. "I do," or "Her mother and I do."*

He then takes the bride's right hand and places it in the groom's left hand, and retires to his place and is seated.

THE MARRIAGE VOWS

The Pastor will invite the bride and groom and their attendants to come forward before the altar. Then the Pastor will say:

"Our Lord Jesus Christ taught us that at the beginning of creation God 'made them male and female.' *For this cause a man shall leave his father and mother and shall cleave to his wife; and the two shall become one flesh. Consequently they are no longer two, but one flesh.*

You have come to be made husband and wife. Will you join hands, and repeat these vows after me?

The groom repeats these vows as the Pastor instructs:

I, G_____, take you, B_____ to be my wife, to have and to hold, from this day forward, for better for worse, for richer for poorer, in sickness and in health, to love and to cherish, until we are parted by death; as God is my witness, I give you my promise.

The bride repeats these vows as the Pastor instructs:

I, B_____, take you, G_____ to be my husband, to have and to hold, from this day forward, for better for worse, for richer for poorer, in sickness and in health, to love and to cherish, until we are parted by death; as God is my witness, I give you my promise.

READING OF SCRIPTURE

The Word of God describes the kind of love we are to have, each for the other: *"love is kind, and is not jealous; love does not brag and is not arrogant, does not act unbecomingly; it does not seek its own, is not provokes, does not take into account a wrong suffered, does not rejoice in unrighteousness,*

but rejoices with the truth; bears all things, believes all things, hope all things, endures all things. "Love never fails." (1 Corinthians 13:4-8). *Having this love in your hearts, you have chosen to seal your vows by the giving and receiving of rings* (a ring).

THE EXCHANGE OF RINGS

The Pastor shall ask for each ring and ask God's blessing as follows:

"Bless, O Lord, this ring to be a sign of the vows by which this man and woman have bound themselves to each other; through Jesus Christ our Lord, Amen!

The giver places the ring on the ring-finger of the other's hand and repeats as the Pastor instructs:

"I give you this ring, as a symbol of my vow, and with all that I am, and all that I have, I honor you; in the name of the Father and of the Son and of the Holy Spirit. Amen.

PRAYER FOR THE BRIDE & GROOM

"Eternal God, creator and preserver of life, author of salvation, and giver of all grace, look with favor upon this man and this woman whom You make one flesh in holy matrimony. Grant that their wills be so knit together in Your will, and that their spirits be so knit with Your Spirit, that they each may grow in love and peace with You and with one another all the days of their lives. Give them grace, when they hurt each other, to recognize and acknowledge their fault, and to seek each other's forgiveness and Yours. Make their life together a sign of Christ's love to this sinful and broken world. Give them such fulfillment and mutual affection that they may reach out in love and concern for others. Grant that all married persons who have witnessed these vows may find their lives strengthen and their loyalties confirmed. (Through Christ our Lord, Amen.)

In place of the sentence in brackets, *"The Lord's Prayer" may be spoken or sung.*

THE PRONOUNCEMENT OF MARRIAGE

Then the Pastor joins the right hands of husband and wife and says:

"Now that G_____ and B_____ have given themselves to each other by solemn vows, before us and before God as witness, and have shown their affection and trust by the giving

and receiving of a ring (rings) *and by joining hands, I pronounce that they are husband and wife, in the name of the Father, and of the Son, and of the Holy Spirit. Therefore what God has put together; let no man pull asunder, in Jesus' name. Amen*

THE NUPTIAL KISS

Then the Pastor shall say to the bridegroom:

You may kiss your bride.

THE BENEDICTION

"Now to Him who is able to keep you from falling, and to present you faultless before the presence of His glory with exceeding joy, to God our Savior, Who alone is wise, be glory and majesty, dominion and power, both now and forever. Amen."

15 A CONTEMPORARY MARRIAGE SERVICE

- <u>STATEMENT OF PURPOSE</u> – *"Friends, we have come today at the invitation of B_____ and G_____ to share in the joy of their wedding. This outward celebration we shall see and hear is an expression of the inner love and devotion they have in their hearts. Jesus Christ reminds us that at the beginning the Creator made us male and female, and said, 'For this cause a man shall leave his father and mother and shall cleave to his wife; and the two shall become one flesh." God loved us, and created us to love to others. Our lives find completion only as we love and are loved in return. Together, we can become what we could never be separately. Marriage is of God. G_____ _____ and B_____ _____ come today desiring to be united in this sacred relationship.*

Or this,

"God is the author of love. The Bible teaches that God is love, and that love comes from God. From beginning to end, the Bible is a love story; and in there we read of God's love for His people, of the love that sent Christ to the cross, of redeeming love for the sinner, of abiding love for the redeemed. We read also of the love of man and

woman: of Jacob's love for Rachel, of Mary pledged to Joseph, of the Shulamite and her beloved. *In the beginning, when the Lord God formed man from the dust of the ground and placed him in the Garden of Eden, Adam was lonely. So the Lord God made a companion and helper for him. When Adam saw Eve, he was no longer lonely. God can lead us to our life's companion.*

Abraham prayed that God would find a wife for his son, Isaac, and God answered that prayer. When Abraham's servant found Rebekah, the servant bowed and worshiped, praising God. Then he brought her to his master's son. The Scripture says, "Isaac loved her, and he was comforted." *God has guided G_____ and B_____ to this moment, has blessed their love and brought them together. Let us again go to Him in prayer.* 'O God, You have made us male and female, and given us the desire to leave father and mother and be united to the one we love and to become one flesh. We thank You for the love G_____ and B_____ have for You. We believe that You have led them to this day, and we ask Your blessing as they exchange their vows and seal their promises. As they become husband and wife, may they do so not only in our presence, but in Yours, with Your grace surrounding them and Your love within their hearts. We pray through Christ, Amen.

DECLARATION OF INTENT

TO GROOM: *G_____ _____ , do you now leave your father and mother to establish your own home with B_____ as her husband, to receive her as your wife, to make a home where she will be loved and cared for as long as God grants her life? If so, answer, "I DO."*

TO BRIDE: *B_____ _____, do you now leave your father and mother to establish your own home with G_____ as wife, to receive him as your husband, to make a home where he will be loved and cared for as long as God grants him life? If so, answer, "I DO."*

TO PARENTS OF BOTH BRIDE & GROOM *(Bride's mother, groom's parents will stand): "Do you promise to encourage G_____ and B_____ in their marriage, to present an example love and devotion for them to emulate, and to help them build a strong and stable home for themselves and their family? If so, answer, "WE DO."*

TO THE BRIDE'S FATHER: *"Who is giving this woman to be married to this man?* Bride's father answers, *"I do,"* or, *"Her mother and I do,"* then places bride's right hand in the groom's left. Bride's father takes his place by his wife and they and groom's parents are seated.

EXHORTATION TO BRIDE & GROOM

*If the wedding couple and their attendants are to move to
the platform, they do so at this point.*

The ceremony of marriage in which you come to be
united is the first and oldest ceremony in all the world,
celebrated in the beginning in the presence of God
Himself. Marriage is a gift of God, given to comfort the
sorrows of life and magnify its joys.

Marriage is the clasping of hands, the blending of hearts,
the union of two lives as one. Your marriage must stand,
not by the authority of the State nor by the seal on your
wedding certificate, but by the strength of your love and
by the power of your faith in each other and in God.
You can have this kind of home if you continue to
recognize God as the source of romance and love and
affection, for these are His gifts.

Build your home on a spiritual foundation because with
God, you will have everything; without Him, you will
have nothing. Now, will you please join hands and, to
each other, express your vows of love and devotion.

THE MARRIAGE VOWS

The couple holds hand and faces each other.

TO GROOM: *G_____, will you repeat this vow to
B_____, saying after me: "I, G_____, take
you, B_____, to be my wife, to have and to hold,*

from this day forward; for better, for worse; for richer, for poorer; in sickness and in health; to love and to cherish until we are separated by death; as God is my witness, I give you my promise.

TO BRIDE: *B_____, will you repeat this vow to G_____, saying after me: "I, B_____, take you, G_____, to be my husband, to have and to hold, from this day forward; for better, for worse; for richer, for poorer; in sickness and in health; to love and to cherish until we are separated by death; as God is my witness, I give you my promise.*

Or this,

"Will you join hands.

TO GROOM: *G_____, do you take B_____ to be your wife, to live and love together in the sight of God, so long as you both shall live? If so, answer, "I DO."*

*Some couples prefer to write their own vows, in which case theirs would be substituted for the vows given here. The vows may either be repeated as the Pastor prompts, or they may be recited from memory. The couple may also choose to read their vows.

TO BRIDE: *B_____, do you take G_____ to be your husband, to live and love together in the sight of God, so long as you both shall live? If so, answer, "I*

DO."

READING OF SCRIPTURE

"The Word of God tells us what love is like and what love does: 'Love is patient, love is kind, and is not jealous; love does not brag and is not arrogant, does not act unbecomingly; it does not seek its own, is not provoked, does not take into account a wrong suffered, does not rejoice in unrighteousness, but rejoices with the truth; bears all things, believes all things, hopes all things, endures all things. Love never fails.' *(1 Corinthians 13:4-8)*

"The New Testament reveals that happiness comes from putting the other first, rather than oneself: 'Be subject one to another in the fear of Christ. Wives, be subject to your own husbands, as to the Lord…Husbands, love your wives, just as Christ loved the church and gave Himself up for her…Let each individual among you also love his own wife even as himself; and let the wife see to it that she respect her husband" *(from Ephesians 5)*

"Having this kind of love in your hearts, you have chosen to exchange rings (a ring) *as the sign and seal of the vows you are making today. May I have the ring* (s)?

THE EXCHANGE OF RINGS

While holding the rings *(ring)*, the Pastor shall say,

"Though small in size, these rings are (this ring is) *very large in significance; and although they are made of precious metal, they remind us that love is not cheap nor common; indeed, love may cost us dearly. Made in a circle, their design tells us that love must never come to an end; we must keep it continuous, and as you wear these rings, whether together or apart for a moment, may they be constant reminders of these glad promises you are making today."*

TO GROOM: *G_____, will you take your ring and place it upon the third finger of B_____'s left hand, and repeat after me this promise, saying:* "With this ring, I seal my promise, to be your faithful and loving husband, as God is my witness."

TO BRIDE: *B_____, will you take your ring and place it upon the third finger of G_____'s left hand, and repeat after me this promise, saying:* "With this ring, I seal my promise, to be your faithful and loving wife, as God is my witness."

LIGHTING THE UNITY CANDLE

Then the Pastor shall say;

"The two outside candles have been lighted to represent your lives to this moment. They are two distinct lights, each capable of going its separate way. To bring joy and radiance into your home, there must be the merging of these two flames into one. From this time onward may

your thoughts be for each other rather than for your individual selves; may your plans be mutual, your joys and sorrows shared. As you each take a candle and together light the center one, you will extinguish your own candles, thus having the center candle represent the union of your two lives into one flesh.

As this center light cannot be divided, let not your lives be divided, but instead be the united testimony of a Christian home, as Christ gives you light.

Three candles have been arranged on a table nearby; center candle unlit, two outer candles burning – see instructions under THE FORMAL WEDDING / LIGHTING THE CANDLES.

When the Pastor says, *"As you each take a candle..."* the couple comes forward, each taking one of the outer candles and together lighting center candle. They extinguish their individual candles and step back to their places. Caution the bride to keep her veil from the flames.

PRAYER FOR THE BRIDE & GROOM

"Our Father, we come today asking Your blessing upon these two lives and this home being established. You have made us so that we are incomplete without the other so that we yearn for someone whom we love and whose love we can receive. We are thankful for the love we see here, and even more, for the love we feel from You. May

we never take Your love for granted.

We pray that Your love will be the shield and stay for G_____ and B_____. When joy comes, may they share it together. When sorrow threatens, may they bear it together. In gladness or in tears, in sunshine or shadow, may they ever draw closer to each other and nearer to You. Grant them patience, gentleness, forbearance, and understanding. O Father, protect their home from those forces that would break it apart. We ask for health, for long life, for the fulfillment of every good dream and may their love continue through life and finally blend into the life eternal.

Through Christ we pray, Amen!

Or this,

"Our Father, source of love and life, these Your children come today asking Your blessing upon their marriage. May theirs be a home of faith and trust, like that of Abraham and Sarah; may theirs be the love that endures, like that of Isaac and Rebekah; may their lives be given in service to Christ, like those of Aquila and Pricilla. May joy and gladness flow from them into the hearts of many others. Guide them in the way of wisdom; lead them along the path of righteousness.

May Your grace be theirs in every joy and sorrow. O Father, may this home be an example of the love of Jesus Christ. We pray in His name, Amen.

*If desired, the Lord's Prayer may be used also.

PRONOUNCEMENT OF MARRIAGE

"You have come before us and before God and have expressed your desire to be husband and wife. You have shown your love and affection by joining hands, have made promises of faith and devotion, each to the other, and have sealed these promises by the giving and receiving of rings (a ring). *I therefore pronounce that you are husband and wife. May God bless you and keep you and give you His peace. Amen.*

Taking their joined hands in his, the Pastor shall; *"What God has put together, let no man pull asunder."*

THE KISS

TO THE GROOM: *You may kiss your bride.*

RECOGNITION OF PARENTS

Some couples give roses to their parents on the way out of the church.

Others prefer to include this in the ceremony. The following is one suggestion as to how this may be done. The Pastor shall say to the audience;

"As G_____ and B_____ begin their lives together and establish their own home, they wish to offer

tokens of appreciation and recognition to the homes from which they came."

The wedding party remains in place as the couple takes roses or other flowers from the table where the unity candle was lighted and presents them as follows: *the groom gives his rose to the bride's mother and he and the bride express informal words of thanks to her parents. The couple moves to the groom's parents where the bride presents a rose to the groom's mother, and the couple expresses informal words of thanks to them. The couple moves back to the platform for the benediction and the presentation.* During the recognition of the parents, the parents, this is where a song may be sang. *(Or not)*

THE BENEDICTION

"The LORD bless you and keep you;

The LORD make His face shine on you,

And be gracious to you;

The LORD life up His countenance on you,

And give you peace.

(Numbers 6:24-26)

ALTERNATIVE BENEDICTION

"But you, beloved, building yourselves up on your most

holy faith, praying in the Holy Spirit, keep yourselves in the love of God, looking for the mercy of our Lord Jesus Christ unto eternal life."

(Jude 20-21)

PRESENTATION OF THE NEWLYWEDS

The couple turns and faces the audience, and the Pastor shall say;

"Dear friends, may I present to you Mr. and Mrs. G_____.

16 PREMARITAL COUNSELING

Some couples only want to plan a wedding, but others are willing to talk about their lives together. These suggestions may be useful during one or more such sessions. Treat them as suggestions only; once the ceremony is decided upon, lay this manual aside and *trust to God's leading.*

Help the couple feel comfortable.

The atmosphere should be that of friends getting together informally, not that of an authority figure issuing lifetime rules, nor an inquisitor probing intimate secrets. The question, *"How did you meet each other?"* is a good opener, and gets them talking about themselves and their relationship. Genuine interest and comments such as, *"What did you think of him at first?"* and, *"When did you start to be serious?"* keep the talk flowing. The session moves to a deeper level with your question, *"How well do you think you know each other?"* Laughing, they may ask, *"What do you mean?"*

Help them explore their knowledge of each other with

questions such as, *"What does he/she like to do more than anything else?"* *"Where would he/she like to go on a vacation?"* and the question, *"What is something you do that really makes him/her unhappy?"* They can talk over their answers, sometimes serious, sometimes not, and in the process learn even more about each other.

Has either party been married before? If there was a divorce, what led to it and will that create problems in this marriage?

What will be their relationship to the former wife or husband?

To the children? If the children from the former marriage will be in this new home, what steps will be taken to make them feel accepted and wanted? There cannot be lingering doubts in the mind of one party concerning the past marriage of the other. Help them discuss these and clear them away. What about health habits? Does either smoke? Drink? Use narcotics? How does the other feel about this?

Emphasize that marriage is not a reform school, that the ceremony itself will do nothing to change such habits. If there is a problem now with drinking, for example, it will not improve automatically after marriage. Ask, *"How will you feel if he keeps on drinking after you're married?"* If need be, force them to face this matter squarely. Help them see the necessity of dealing with such issues now rather than postponing making changing until later. If changes are not made now, in all probability, they will never be made at all. Ask, *"Who will be the brakes and who will be the accelerator?"* This opens up many possibilities *(money, sex, work habits, etc.),* but the question is general enough that it enables them to bring up whatever area they want to discuss.

The subheadings named above *(money, sex, work habits)* are a reflection of their personalities and emotional makeup. Who will be the more active, the more aggressive? Who is more likely to be passive? Will there be a conflict if both husband and wife try to run the house? Or if *"she tries to run things?"* If one person more ambitious, or better educated, than the other? Will this create resentment and cause a growing breach in their marriage? Does he/she have a job? Does she plan to work after marriage? Will they have a place of their own, even if it is a room in an extended stay hotel? If they are to live with parents, what will be the relationship with their in-laws? If the husband were to be offered a better position in a distant city, what would they do? Who will handle the checkbook? Do they plan to have a budget? Which one will be the enforcer? And how strictly? Are there debts that will create financial pressure? Where do their families fit into their relationship? How do the families feel about the coming marriage? Does the couple see possible problems in this area? How do they handle conflict? Has either seen the other angry? At him/her? What caused the trouble, and how did they resolve it?

Who is usually the first to say, *"I'm sorry?"* Will he/she continue having to give in, or will there be mutual awareness when hurt has occurred, and willingness to back up, apologize, and go on? If there has not been up to now, why do they think things will be different once they are married? The way conflict is handled now is *"practice"* for the way they will settle differences later. A problem here does not mean that this couple should not be married, but it does indicate that they need to develop better means of resolving their difficulties. The following questions opens up an important area, no matter what level their physical contact, whether holding hands or living together: *"Do you feel good about what is happening between you physical?"* If they don't know how to respond, you may say, *"Well, no doubt you're expressing you affection.*

I hope you're hugging and kissing each other. The physical is certainly one of God's gifts to a man and woman." The questions go farther: *"Is one the aggressor? Does the other feel like the victim?" "What if it turns out to be like this after you're married?"* They need to explore this area seriously, for the physical expression of love can enrich and satisfy, but the lack of adequate expression can frustrate and lead to resentment,

outbursts of rage, illness, and divorce. Help them see that love does not mean taking, but giving. Do they hope to have children? How many? Have they discussed birth control? Do they have any health problems they need to discuss or take to a physician? Will she plan to work if they have a baby? If not, will she resent staying at home? Do they intend to bring up their children in a Christian home? What steps are they prepared to take toward this goal? Which one has the higher standards? Which one has the deeper commitment to Christ? How often do they plan to attend church? Where? How much do they intend to give to the work of Christ? Are they making these decisions now? What steps do they need to take in order to begin their marriage on a Christian foundation? Offer to help the couple in any way possible as they approach their wedding day. Be positive about the wedding and the marriage, and help them put aside their anxiety enough to enjoy their wedding.

17 RESOURCES

To find out about the state laws for marriages in any particular state, log onto

https://www.weddingwire.com/wedding-ideas/marriage-laws-by-state

Who can perform marriage? Know the guidelines for each state if you are not an ordained minister. Go to this link to find out if you are legal to perform marriages.

https://www.thespruce.com/recognized-marriage-officiants-2300735

ABOUT THE AUTHOR

Dr. Rose White Brown was born in Philadelphia, Pennsylvania. She has had the opportunity to travel and has resided in various states and has even lived 2 years abroad in the Republic of South Africa.

She holds a Bachelors of Theology, Masters of Divinity and holds an Honorary Doctorate Degree in Divinity. She has attended Faith Theological in Tampa, Florida, Liberty University and Grand Canyon University.

Dr. Brown is a licensed and ordained minister, having served in many ministerial roles since 1978. She went into full time ministry in 2003 serving men and women worldwide. Her business background is in Medical Office and Business Management for 35 years.

She is an author and writer, wife, mother, radio broadcast host, spiritual mother, mentor and Life Coach. She is the founder of several ministries and organizations and the president and founder of Wise Business Choices, Inc.

Learn more about the organization and all that
Dr. Brown supports by visiting
www.kogfellowshipchurch.org.

$11.95   *Rose Brown Ministries*
ISBN: 1096771678
ISBN-13: 9781096771678